The Women's Institute

celebration
cupcakes

Kim Morphew

SIMON &
SCHUSTER
ILLUSTRATED

London · New York · Sydney · Toronto

A CBS COMPANY

First published in Great Britain
by Simon & Schuster UK Ltd, 2011
A CBS Company

Copyright © WI Enterprises Ltd, 2011

Simon & Schuster
Illustrated Books,
Simon & Schuster UK Ltd, 1st Floor,
222 Gray's Inn Road, London WC1X 8HB

1 2 3 4 5 6 7 8 9 10

Editorial Director: **Francine Lawrence**
Commercial Director: **Ami Richards**
Senior Commissioning Editor: **Nicky Hill**
Project Editor: **Nicki Lampon**
Designer: **Fiona Andreanelli**
Food Photographer: **Lis Parsons**
Stylist: **Tony Hutchinson**
Home Economist: **Kim Morphew**

Colour reproduction by **Dot Gradations Ltd, UK**
Printed and bound in China

A CIP catalogue for this book is
available from the British Library.

ISBN 978-0-85720-233-8

Notes on the recipes

Both metric and imperial measurements have been
given in all recipes. Use one set of measurements only
and not a mixture of both. Spoon measures are level
and 1 tablespoon = 15 ml, 1 teaspoon = 5 ml.

Preheat ovens before use and cook on the centre shelf
unless cooking more than one item. If using a fan oven,
reduce the heat by 10–20°C, but check with your handbook.

Medium eggs have been used.

This book contains recipes made with nuts. Those with known
allergic reactions to nuts and nut derivatives, pregnant and
breast-feeding women and very young children should avoid
these dishes.

Stockists

COOK IN THYME
Cook In Thyme, 22 Upper High Street, Epsom,
Surrey KT17 4QR
www.cookinthyme.co.uk
01372 740 653

JANE ASHER PARTY CAKES AND SUGARCRAFT
22–24 Cale Street, London SW3 3QU
www.janeasher.com
020 7584 6177

On the web
www.squires-shop.com (0845 6171 810)
www.cakescookiesandcraftsshop.co.uk
www.surbitonart.co.uk
www.edible-glitter.co.uk

Contents

Introduction

Small and beautiful cakes have been popular throughout history, and in this book you'll find everything you need to know about making their most chic and fashionable incarnation – cupcakes.

Quick to make, simple to decorate and elegant to eat, beautifully iced cupcakes are simply divine when displayed on a cake stand and make a creative and original surprise for a birthday, anniversary or wedding celebration.

Even if you've never baked a cake before, making cupcakes is a wonderfully easy way to start – our step-by-step recipes will show you how, with plenty of suggestions on how to decorate them for your party. And making cupcakes with children is the perfect way to introduce them to baking. Children love their size and can let their imaginations run riot when decorating them.

Experienced cooks will find inspiration and practical advice here too – from how to make stunning cupcakes for a wedding to plenty of hints and tips for adding your own special touch.

So go on, have a go and have fun.

Basic cupcakes

Rich chocolate cupcakes

Makes 12
Preparation time: 15 minutes + cooling
Cooking time: 18–20 minutes

75 g (2¾ oz) **unsalted butter**, softened
150 g (5½ oz) **caster sugar**
2 **eggs**
50 g (1¾ oz) **self-raising flour**
100 g (3½ oz) **plain flour**
½ teaspoon **bicarbonate of soda**
40 g (1½ oz) **cocoa powder**, sieved
150 ml (5½ fl oz) **buttermilk**

Preheat the oven to 180°C/350°F/Gas Mark 4. Line a 12-hole muffin tin with paper muffin cases.

Whisk the butter and sugar together using an electric hand whisk or beat with a wooden spoon until pale and creamy. Gradually whisk in the eggs until just combined. Then add both flours, the bicarbonate of soda, cocoa powder and buttermilk, whisking until combined and fluffy.

Divide equally between the paper cases, filling them about two-thirds full, and bake in the oven for 18–20 minutes until golden and risen. Leave to cool in the tin for 5 minutes, then transfer to a wire rack to go cold.

Variations
Chocolate chip: Stir through 50 g (1¾ oz) of white, dark or milk chocolate chips after adding the flour.

Mocha: Stir through 1 tablespoon of instant coffee granules, dissolved in 1 tablespoon of boiling water, along with the buttermilk.

Zesty lemon cupcakes

Makes 12
Preparation time: 15 minutes + cooling
Cooking time: 18–20 minutes

175 g (6 oz) **unsalted butter**, softened
175 g (6 oz) **caster sugar**
3 **eggs**
175 g (6 oz) **self-raising flour**, sieved
zest of 1 large **lemon**
½ teaspoon **baking powder**
2 tablespoons **milk**

Preheat the oven to 190°C/375°F/Gas Mark 5. Line a 12-hole muffin tin with paper muffin cases.

Whisk the butter and sugar together using an electric hand whisk or beat with a wooden spoon until pale and creamy. Gradually whisk in the eggs until just combined. Then add the flour, lemon zest, baking powder and milk. Whisk until combined and fluffy.

Divide equally between the paper cases, filling them about two-thirds full, and bake in the oven for 18–20 minutes until golden and risen. Leave to cool in the tin for 5 minutes, then transfer to a wire rack to go cold.

Variations
Zesty orange: Replace the lemon zest with the grated zest of 1 orange.

Lime and coconut: Replace the lemon zest with the grated zest of 1 lime and add 25 g (1 oz) of desiccated coconut along with the flour.

Poppy seed: Use either orange or lemon zest and add 1 tablespoon of poppy seeds.

Truly vanilla cupcakes

Makes 12
Preparation time: 15 minutes + cooling
Cooking time: 18–20 minutes

125 g (4½ oz) **unsalted butter**, softened
175 g (6 oz) **caster sugar**
1 **vanilla pod**, cut in half and seeds scraped out or
    1 tablespoon **vanilla extract**
3 **eggs**
125 g (4½ oz) **self-raising flour**, sieved
50 g (1¾ oz) '00' grade **plain flour**, sieved
75 ml (3 fl oz) **buttermilk**

Preheat the oven to 190°C/375°F/Gas Mark 5. Line a 12-hole muffin tin with paper muffin cases.

Whisk the butter, sugar and vanilla seeds together using an electric hand whisk or beat with a wooden spoon until pale and creamy. Add the eggs, flours and buttermilk and whisk until combined and fluffy.

Divide equally between the paper cases, filling them about two-thirds full, and bake in the oven for 18–20 minutes until golden and risen. Leave to cool in the tin for 5 minutes, then transfer to a wire rack to go cold.

Variations
Marbled chocolate: At the end of step 2 put half the mixture into another bowl. Stir in 2 tablespoons of sieved cocoa powder. Return the cocoa mixture to the vanilla mixture and gently fold once or twice to marble together. Finish as step 3.

Raspberry swirl: Mash 100 g (3½ oz) of fresh raspberries in a bowl until you have a rough purée. At the end of step 2, fold through the purée until just mixed and slightly marbled. Continue as above.

White chocolate chip: Stir through 50 g (1¾ oz) of white chocolate chips at the end of step 2.

Carrot cupcakes

Makes 12
Preparation time: 20 minutes + cooling
Cooking time: 20 minutes

150 g (5½ oz) **carrots**, peeled
50 g (1¾ oz) **raisins** or **sultanas**
200 g (7 oz) **self-raising flour**, sieved
½ teaspoon **bicarbonate of soda**
150 g (5½ oz) **light muscovado sugar**
zest of 1 **orange**
½ teaspoon **ground mixed spice**
3 **eggs**
100 ml (3½ fl oz) **sunflower oil**
75 ml (3 fl oz) **buttermilk**

Preheat the oven to 190°C/375°F/Gas Mark 5. Line a 12-hole muffin tin with paper muffin cases.

Coarsely grate the carrots into a large bowl. Add the raisins, flour, bicarbonate of soda, sugar, orange zest and mixed spice. Lightly beat together the eggs, oil and buttermilk in a jug until combined. Pour the egg mixture into the flour and stir with a spatula until just combined.

Divide equally between the paper cases and bake in the oven for 20 minutes until lightly golden and risen. Leave to cool in the tin for 5 minutes, then transfer to a wire rack to go cold.

Variations
Courgette and chocolate: Replace the carrots with 150 g (5½ oz) of grated courgettes and use 175 g (6 oz) of self-raising flour, adding 25 g (1 oz) of sieved cocoa powder to the flour. Omit the raisins and orange zest.

Beetroot and cranberry: Replace the carrots with 150 g (5½ oz) of peeled, raw, grated beetroot and replace the raisins with 50 g (1¾ oz) of dried cranberries. Omit the mixed spice.

Coffee and almond cupcakes

Makes **12**
Preparation time: **15 minutes + cooling**
Cooking time: **20–25 minutes**

2 tablespoons instant **coffee** granules
50 ml (2 fl oz) warm **milk**
175 g (6 oz) **unsalted butter**, softened
150 g (5½ oz) **self-raising flour**, sieved
175 g (6 oz) **light brown soft sugar**
3 **eggs**
½ teaspoon **baking powder**
100 g (3½ oz) **ground almonds**

Preheat the oven to 190°C/375°F/Gas Mark 5. Line a 12-hole muffin tin with paper muffin cases.

Dissolve the coffee granules in the warm milk. Put the butter, flour, sugar, eggs, baking powder and ground almonds in a large bowl. Add the coffee milk and whisk together using an electric hand whisk or beat with a wooden spoon until pale and creamy.

Divide equally between the paper cases and bake in the oven for 20–25 minutes until golden and risen. Leave to cool in the tin for 5 minutes, then transfer to a wire rack to go cold.

Variations

Totally almond: Replace the coffee granules with 1 teaspoon of almond extract. There is no need to warm the milk. Just add with all the other ingredients.

Totally nuts: Omit the coffee granules, simply whizz 100 g (3½ oz) of walnuts, pecans or hazelnuts and use them instead of the ground almonds.

Gorgeous ginger cupcakes

Makes **12**
Preparation time: **20 minutes + cooling**
Cooking time: **18–20 minutes**

200 g (7 oz) **unsalted butter**
75 g (2¾ oz) **dark muscovado sugar**
100 g (3½ oz) **golden syrup**
175 g (6 oz) **self-raising flour**
¼ teaspoon **bicarbonate of soda**
2 teaspoons **ground ginger**
30 g (1¼ oz) **glacé ginger**, finely chopped
3 **eggs**, beaten

Preheat the oven to 190°C/375°F/Gas Mark 5. Line a 12-hole muffin tin with paper muffin cases.

Put the butter, sugar and golden syrup into a large bowl and beat together until smooth and creamy. Add the flour, bicarbonate of soda, ground ginger, glacé ginger and eggs and whisk with an electric hand whisk or beat with a wooden spoon until combined.

Divide equally between the paper cases and bake in the oven for 18–20 minutes until golden and risen. Leave to cool in the tin for 5 minutes, then transfer to a wire rack to go cold.

Variations

Golden syrup: Use 75 g (2¾ oz) of light brown soft sugar instead of the dark muscovado and omit the ground and glacé ginger.

Spiced cupcakes: Replace the ground ginger with 2 teaspoons of ground mixed spice, and the glacé ginger with 30 g (1¼ oz) of finely chopped candied peel.

Basic cupcake frostings

Buttercream

To ice 12 cupcakes
Preparation time: 10 minutes

125 g (4½ oz) **unsalted butter**, softened
250 g (9 oz) **icing sugar**, sieved
2 tablespoons **boiled water**, cooled

Whisk the butter in a bowl until fluffy. Gradually add the icing sugar and whisk until it comes together. Add the water and whisk until light and fluffy. Use as required.

Variations
Replace the water with the following:

Lemon – use the juice of 1 large lemon

Orange – use the juice of ½ an orange

Vanilla – use 2 teaspoons of vanilla extract

Coffee – dissolve 1 tablespoon of instant coffee granules in 2 tablespoons of boiling water

Chocolate – mix 2 tablespoons of cocoa powder with 2 tablespoons of boiling water

Cream cheese frosting

To ice 12 cupcakes
Preparation time: 10 minutes

200 g (7 oz) **icing sugar**, sieved
150 g (5½ oz) **full fat cream cheese**
50 g (1¾ oz) **Quark**
50 g (1¾ oz) **unsalted butter**, softened

In a bowl, mix together the icing sugar, cream cheese, Quark and butter until you have a smooth icing. Use as required.

Variations
Lemon or Lime: Add the grated zest of 1 lemon or lime.

Orange: Add the grated zest of ½ an orange.

Vanilla: Add the seeds from ½ a vanilla pod.

Marshmallow icing

To ice 12 cupcakes
Preparation time: 15 minutes + cooling

1 large **egg white**
a pinch of **cream of tartar**
60 g (2 oz) **caster sugar**
75 g (2¾ oz) **mini white marshmallows**

Put the egg white and cream of tartar in a heatproof bowl. Whisk until soft peaks form using an electric hand whisk. Then gradually whisk in the sugar until you have a glossy meringue and the sugar has dissolved.

Put the bowl over a pan of simmering water and add the marshmallows. Whisk continuously for about 5 minutes until the marshmallows have nearly melted.

Remove from the heat and whisk for a further 5 minutes until the marshmallows have completely melted and the mixture thickens sufficiently. Leave to cool for 15 minutes, stirring occasionally until the mixture stands in soft peaks. Use as required.

Glacé icing

To ice 12 cupcakes
Preparation time: 5 minutes

300 g (10½ oz) **icing sugar**, sieved
2 teaspoons **unsalted butter**, melted
1–2 tablespoons **boiled water**, cooled

Put the icing sugar and butter in a bowl and gradually stir in the water until you get a smooth, thick icing. Use as required.

Variations

Chocolate glacé icing: Omit the water. In a small pan gradually mix 100 ml (3½ fl oz) of milk into 50 g (1¾ oz) of cocoa powder until smooth. Gently heat until hot. Then stir into the icing sugar and butter.

Passion fruit icing: Replace the water with the sieved juice from 1–2 ripe passion fruit.

Coffee icing: Dissolve 1 tablespoon of instant coffee granules in the boiling water. Allow to cool before using.

Lemon icing: Use the juice of ½ a lemon instead of the water.

Royal icing

To ice 12 cupcakes
Preparation time: 5 minutes

5 tablespoons **cold water**
500 g (1 lb 2 oz) **royal icing sugar**

Put the water into a bowl and add the icing sugar. Whisk for 5 minutes using an electric hand whisk until you get firm peaks. Use as required.

Chocolate ganache

To ice 12 cupcakes
Preparation time: 15 minutes

75 ml (3 fl oz) **double cream**
25 g (1 oz) **unsalted butter**
200 g (7 oz) **dark chocolate**, finely chopped
100 g (3½ oz) **white chocolate**, finely chopped

Put the cream, butter and both chocolates in a heatproof bowl and place over a pan of barely simmering water. Gently heat until the chocolate and butter have melted, stirring occasionally. Remove from the heat and use as required.

Variation
White chocolate ganache: Omit the dark chocolate and use 300 g (10½ oz) of white chocolate.

Runny fondant icing

To ice 12 cupcakes
Preparation time: 5 minutes

300 g (10½ oz) fondant **icing sugar**, sieved
approx. 3 tablespoons **cold water**

Put the icing sugar in a bowl and gradually stir in the water until you get a smooth thick icing. Use as required.

Variation
If you want, why not flavour royal icing or runny fondant icing by using 4 tablespoons of fruit juice instead of the water.

Cupcake know-how

Piping bags and nozzles

You can use traditional reusable piping bags when decorating cupcakes but plastic disposable piping bags are recommended. Not only are they easier and more hygienic to use as they can be thrown away afterwards, you can snip off the end of the piping bag, making it easy to ice cupcakes if you don't have a nozzle. Remember to recycle them if possible.

Nozzles or icing tips come in a range of sizes from fine writing nozzles to large nozzles for stars, basketwork, leaves and petals. Generally the smaller the nozzle the thinner the icing will be. To start piping, fill the piping bag only two-thirds full and twist and fold the top of the bag over. If you overfill the piping bag it will seep out the top.

How to colour icing

Food colourings are available in liquid, powder or paste form. Add minute amounts with the tip of a cocktail stick until the desired colour is reached. If you use the liquid colourings you may need to add a little extra sieved icing sugar to the icing, as the liquid will thin it.

How to ice a cupcake with a palette knife

1. Scoop some buttercream or frosting on to a palette knife and place in the centre of the cupcake.

2. Angling the palette knife, work the buttercream or frosting out to one edge of the cupcake by gently pushing it using small strokes.

3. Turn the cupcake and repeat the process, smoothing the joins with a little more buttercream or frosting.

4. Use the tip of the palette knife to create swirls in the top. Decorate as desired.

How to pipe a swirl

1. Use a large or small star nozzle depending on the thickness you desire and put into the end of a disposable piping bag.

2. Half fill the icing bag with buttercream, frosting or icing.

3. Hold the cupcake with one hand to steady it, and then hold the icing bag almost upright with your other hand.

4. Starting at the outside edge, place the nozzle just above the cake. Gently squeeze the bag, moving the bag in a circular motion, working inwards and upwards to make a spiral, slightly overlapping the icing.

5. To finish, simply lift the piping bag off and pull away from the cake. Decorate as desired.

Tip If you want smaller swirls, use the same technique but use a smaller star nozzle and work in smaller circles over the top of the cake.

Storing cupcakes

Cupcakes can be stored in an airtight tin or plastic container for 3–5 days. If they have an icing of fresh cream or cream cheese they should be kept in the fridge in a plastic container for up to 3 days.

Freezing cupcakes

Once baked, you can freeze un-iced cupcakes when they are completely cold. Simply open freeze until frozen and then put into freezer bags. Defrost for about 1 hour, then ice as required. If the cupcake has a buttercream icing it can be frozen iced, as above, and then defrosted before finally decorating.

Birthday balloon cupcakes

You can use any sweets you like, just as long as they look like balloons.

Makes 12
Decorating time:
 20 minutes

52.5 g packet **fruit pastilles**
2 **strawberry laces**
1 quantity **Lemon glacé icing** (see variation, page 12)
12 **Zesty lemon cupcakes** (see page 6)

Carefully cut each fruit pastille in half horizontally using a sharp knife, and cut the strawberry laces into short lengths.

Using a small palette knife, spread the glace icing all over the top of the cakes, smoothing it down as you go. Let the icing settle for a few minutes.

Decorate each cupcake with two or three fruit pastilles and arrange a strawberry lace per fruit pastille to look like a balloon. Leave to set.

Tips Most supermarkets have their own range of 'retro' style sweets like strawberry laces, but if not then any good local newsagent should stock them. To finish the look, use 'happy birthday' style candles.

Orange or lime glacé icing also works well with these cupcakes, just replace the lemon juice in the icing with the same quantity of orange or lime juice.

Little pirate cupcakes

Every little boy dreams of being a pirate so why not make him the captain and his birthday cake the crew!

Makes 12
Decorating time:
  45 minutes

300 g (10½ oz) **ready-to-roll white fondant icing**
12 **Zesty lemon cupcakes** (see page 6)
50 g (1¾ oz) **apricot jam**, melted
75 g (2¾ oz) **ready-to-roll black fondant icing**
boiled water, cooled
75 g (2¾ oz) **ready-to-roll red fondant icing**
50 g (1¾ oz) **butter**, softened
100 g (3½ oz) **icing sugar**, sieved, plus extra for dusting
black food colouring

Equipment
6.5 cm (2½ inch) round cutter
6 cm (2¼ inch) round cutter
disposable piping bags
plain writing nozzle

Lightly dust a clean work surface with a little icing sugar. Roll out the white fondant icing until about 3–4 mm (⅛–¼ inch) thick. Using a 6.5 cm (2½ inch) round cookie cutter, stamp out 12 circles. You may need to re-roll the icing.

Brush the tops of the cupcakes with the apricot jam then put a white circle on to the top of each cupcake, lightly pressing down.

Roll out the black fondant icing until about 3–4 mm (⅛–¼ inch) thick and stamp out three circles using a 6 cm (2¼ inch) round cookie cutter. Cut each circle in half to make six semi-circles. Lightly brush the underside of each semi-circle with cooled boiled water and place on the top half of six cupcakes to look like a hat. Using the trimmings, cut out 12 very small triangles and arrange to one side of the semi-circles to look like ties. Repeat with the red fondant icing and the remaining cupcakes.

Put the butter into a bowl and whisk until fluffy. Gradually add the icing sugar and about 1–2 teaspoons of cooled boiled water and whisk until light and fluffy. Put half the buttercream into a piping bag with a writing nozzle and pipe small dots over the red hats and skull and crossbones over the black hats.

Squeeze any excess buttercream back into the bowl and wash out the nozzle. Colour the remaining buttercream black, put into a piping bag with the writing nozzle and pipe an eye patch, an eye and a mouth over each pirate.

Little princess cupcakes

Perfect for any little girl's birthday. If you like you can use non-edible butterfly cake toppers (see stockists, page 2).

Makes 12
Decorating time:
30 minutes

1 quantity **Lemon buttercream** (see variation, page 10)
red food colouring
blue food colouring
green food colouring
12 **Zesty lemon cupcakes** (see page 6)
12 ready-made **edible wafer daisies**
6 ready-made **sugar butterfly decorations**

Equipment
disposable piping bag
small star nozzle

Divide the buttercream in half and put in separate bowls. Colour one half pink using a few drops of red food colouring and beating with a spatula until the right shade. Colour the remaining buttercream using the blue and green food colouring until you get a turquoise colour, beating again with a spatula.

Spread a little of the pink buttercream over the tops of six cupcakes using a small palette knife. Repeat with the turquoise buttercream and the remaining six cupcakes.

Put the pink buttercream into a piping bag with a small star nozzle and pipe a star border around the edge of each pink cupcake. Repeat with the turquoise buttercream. Decorate each cupcake with a wafer daisy and then choose six to have butterflies as well.

Birthday present cupcakes

Look out for multicoloured fizzy belt sweets in newsagents or sweet shops, or use anything similar that can be bent.

Makes 12
Decorating time:
  30 minutes + 1 hour
  setting

12 **multicoloured fizzy belt sweets** (approx 25 x 2 cm /10 x ¾ inch)
1 quantity **Marshmallow icing** (see page 12)
12 **Carrot cupcakes** (see page 7)
edible pastel pink glitter

Equipment
disposable piping bag
large star nozzle

Cut six sweets in half. Cut a further two sweets in half lengthways, then cut each thin length into three short lengths. To make a bow, take a sweet half and fold in half, but so the join is in the middle. Take a short length and wrap it around the join a few times, quite tightly. Repeat to make 12 bows.

To make ribbon tails, cut each of the remaining four sweets in half lengthways, then cut each of these in to three to make 24 short thin strips. Cut a small triangle out of one end of a strip, to give you a fork like the tail of a ribbon. Repeat with the remaining strips.

Put the marshmallow icing into a piping bag with a large star nozzle and pipe zigzag patterns or large swirls over the top of each cupcake, starting from the outside edge and working your way to the centre.

Put two thin ribbon tails on top of each cupcake, then top each with a bow. Sprinkle with a little glitter and leave to set for 1 hour.

Tip If you like, you could make the ribbon bows out of coloured, ready-to-roll fondant icing instead.

Dotty name cupcakes

Chocolate beans are a great and easy way to decorate cakes. You can also use mini Smarties or small dragées instead.

Makes 12
Preparation and decorating time:
   30 minutes + cooling
Cooking time:
   20 minutes

Cinnamon cupcakes
125 ml (4 fl oz) **Guinness**
150 g (5½ oz) **dark brown soft sugar**
150 g (5½ oz) **unsalted butter**, melted
¼ teaspoon **bicarbonate of soda**
225 g (8 oz) **self-raising flour**
2 teaspoons **ground cinnamon**
3 **eggs**, beaten

To decorate
1 quantity **Buttercream** (see page 10)
edible cream glitter
chocolate beans or **mini Smarties**

Preheat the oven to 180°C/350°F/Gas Mark 4. Line a 12-hole muffin tin with paper muffin cases.

Put the Guinness, sugar and butter in a small pan and gently heat until combined. Stir in the bicarbonate of soda and leave to cool.

Meanwhile put the flour and cinnamon in a bowl. Add the eggs and stir with a spatula until combined. Gradually stir in the cooked Guinness mixture until combined, beating well between each addition.

Transfer to a jug and divide between the paper cases. Bake in the oven for 20 minutes until golden and risen. Leave to cool in the tin for 5 minutes, then transfer to a wire rack to go cold.

Using a small palette knife, spread the buttercream over the tops of the cupcakes until covered. Sprinkle the tops of the cakes with a little edible glitter. Using the chocolate beans, spell out 'Happy Birthday' or the name of the person with a birthday, using each cupcake as one or two letters.

Tip You may wish to make double the batch so that you can spell out 'Happy Birthday' and the person's name.

Sparkly star cupcakes

This works well with other shapes too. Just choose your favourite cookie cutter or pipe freehand designs.

Makes 12
Decorating time:
30 minutes

300 g (10½ oz) **ready-to-roll white fondant icing**
50 g (1¾ oz) **apricot jam**, melted
12 **Carrot cupcakes** (see page 7)
50 g (1¾ oz) **unsalted butter**, softened
100 g (3½ oz) **icing sugar**, sieved, plus extra for dusting
1–2 teaspoons **boiled water**, cooled
hundreds and thousands

Equipment
6.5 cm (2½ inch) round cutter
disposable piping bag
plain writing nozzle
star cookie cutter

Lightly dust a clean work surface with a little icing sugar. Roll out the fondant icing until about 3–4 mm (⅛–¼ inch) thick. Then, using a 6.5 cm (2½ inch) round cookie cutter, stamp out 12 circles. You may need to re-roll the icing. Brush the tops of the cupcakes with the apricot jam then put a white circle on to the top of each cupcake, lightly pressing down.

Put the butter into a bowl and whisk until fluffy. Gradually add the icing sugar and water and whisk until light and fluffy. Put the buttercream into a piping bag with a plain writing nozzle.

Press a small star cookie cutter into the top of each cupcake to score the star shape into the icing. Using this as a guide, pipe around the edge of the star and then fill in with buttercream.

Sprinkle the stars all over with hundred and thousands, shaking off any excess.

18th birthday cupcakes

You could also use 21st keys for a 21st birthday. Plastic number keys can be found from most cake shops or party shops.

Makes 12
Decorating time:
   30 minutes

125 g (4½ oz) **unsalted butter**, softened
250 g (9 oz) **golden icing sugar**, sieved
2 tablespoons **boiled water**, cooled
12 **Coffee and almond cupcakes** (see page 8)
6 **non-edible plastic silver 18th number keys**
small edible silver balls
large edible silver balls
   (see stockists, page 2)

Equipment
disposable piping bag
shell nozzle

Put the butter into a bowl and whisk until fluffy. Gradually add the icing sugar and whisk until it comes together. Add the water and whisk until light and fluffy.

Put the buttercream into a piping bag with a shell nozzle and pipe shells on the cupcakes, starting on the outside edge and working your way to the centre to cover the tops.

Decorate six cupcakes with a silver key and a few small silver balls. Decorate the remaining cupcakes with large and small silver balls. Leave to set.

Tip If you prefer, you can use gold plastic keys and gold edible balls.

40th birthday cupcakes

These make the perfect cakes for any landmark birthday. Just change the number as required.

Makes 12
Decorating time:
  30 minutes

icing sugar, for dusting
75 g (2¾ oz) **ready-to-roll**
  white fondant icing
silver or **snowflake edible**
  dust
1 quantity **Orange**
  buttercream (see
  variation, page 10)
12 **Zesty orange cupcakes**
  (see variation, page 6)
edible silver stars
edible silver balls

Equipment
small brush
disposable piping bags
large star nozzle
plain writing nozzle
4 cm (1½ inch) round cutter

Lightly dust a clean work surface with a little icing sugar. Roll out the fondant icing until about 3–4 mm (⅛–¼ inch) thick. Then, using a 4 cm (1½ inch) round cookie cutter, stamp out 12 circles. Put a little of the silver dust on to a small plate and then brush over the top of each circle using a clean brush. Set aside.

Reserve 2 tablespoons of the buttercream. Put the remaining buttercream into a piping bag with a large star nozzle. Pipe large swirls, starting from the outside edge and working your way to the centre, on top of each cupcake.

Top each buttercream swirl with a silver circle, lightly pressing down. Put the reserved buttercream into a piping bag with a plain writing nozzle and pipe the number '40' on to the circle on six cupcakes. Sprinkle these cakes with silver stars.

Finally, pipe small dots around the edges of the circles on the remaining cakes and sprinkle with silver balls.

60th birthday cupcakes

You can buy embossers from most cake shops but you can also use ink stamps. As long as they are new, they work really well.

Makes 12
Decorating time:
30 minutes

300 g (10½ oz) **ready-to-roll white fondant icing**
gold edible dust
50 g (1¾ oz) **unsalted butter**, softened
100 g (3½ oz) **icing sugar**, plus extra for dusting
1 tablespoon **stem ginger syrup**
12 **Gorgeous ginger cupcakes** (see page 8)
50 g (1¾ oz) **apricot jam**, melted

Equipment
6.5 cm (2½ inch) round cutter
small brush
happy birthday and fleur-de-lis embossing tools
disposable piping bag
plain writing nozzle

Lightly dust a clean work surface with a little icing sugar. Roll out the fondant icing until about 5 mm (¼ inch) thick. Then, using a 6.5 cm (2½ inch) round cookie cutter, stamp out 12 circles.

Put a little of the gold dust on a small plate and then brush over the top of each circle using a clean brush. Using an embossing tool, stamp 'happy birthday' and a fleurs-de-lis on each fondant circle. Using the cookie cutter again, re-stamp out the circles to make sure they are neat.

Put the butter into a bowl and whisk until fluffy. Gradually add the icing sugar and whisk until it comes together. Add the ginger syrup and whisk until light and fluffy.

Brush the tops of the cupcakes with the apricot jam and arrange a fondant circle on each, pressing down lightly. Put the buttercream into a piping bag with a writing nozzle and pipe small dots around the edges of the circles.

Tip You can use any edible lustre powder or dust you like – it's entirely up to you.

Black Forest cupcakes

Store in an airtight container in the fridge for up to 3 days.
For adults, why not add a splash of cassis to the whipped cream?

Makes 12
Decorating time:
  20 minutes

12 **Rich chocolate
  cupcakes** (see page 6)
75 g (2¾ oz) **black cherry jam**
200 ml (7 fl oz) **double cream**
3–4 tablespoons **icing
  sugar**, sieved
100 g (3½ oz) **flaked
  almonds**, toasted
12 whole fresh **cherries**

Using a small serrated knife, cut a cone shape from the top of each cupcake. Put a little cherry jam into the hole in each cake and replace the cones.

Whisk the cream with an electric hand whisk until soft peaks form. Stir through the icing sugar to taste.

Reserve about 4 tablespoons of cream. Using a small palette knife, spread the remaining cream over the tops of the cupcakes until covered. Scatter with the flaked almonds, ensuring an even covering.

Put a small dollop of the reserved cream on top of each cupcake and top each with a fresh cherry. Chill in the fridge until required.

Tip If fresh cherries are out of season, then use frozen stoned cherries. Simply defrost, then pat dry on kitchen towel before using to decorate the cakes.

Teens birthday cupcakes

Ready-made chocolate letters and numbers are available from most large supermarkets. Use them to spell out a name and age.

Makes 12
Preparation and decorating time:
  30 minutes + cooling
Cooking time:
  18–20 minutes

175 g (6 oz) **unsalted butter**, softened
175 g (6 oz) **caster sugar**
3 **eggs**
125 g (4½ oz) **self-raising flour**, sieved
25 g (1 oz) **cocoa powder**, sieved
1 teaspoon **baking powder**
100 g (3½ oz) **ground almonds**
1 teaspoon **vanilla extract**

To decorate
1 quantity **Buttercream** (see page 10)
15 g (½ oz) **cocoa powder**, sieved
ready-made **chocolate letters and numbers**
chocolate vermicelli
edible gold glitter

Equipment
disposable piping bag
large star nozzle

Preheat the oven to 190°C/375°F/Gas Mark 5. Line a 12-hole muffin tin with paper muffin cases.

Whisk the butter and sugar together using an electric hand whisk or beat with a wooden spoon until pale and creamy. Gradually whisk in the eggs until just combined. Add the flour, cocoa powder, baking powder, ground almonds and vanilla extract. Whisk until combined and fluffy.

Divide equally between the paper cases and bake in the oven for 18–20 minutes until golden and risen. Leave to cool in the tin for 5 minutes, then transfer to a wire rack to go cold.

Put half the buttercream in a bowl. Whisk in the cocoa powder until combined. Fill a piping bag with a large star nozzle with alternating spoonfuls of the plain and chocolate buttercreams. Use to pipe large swirls on top of each cake. Decorate with the chocolate numbers and letters, then sprinkle with the vermicelli and gold glitter.

Rocky road cupcakes

This totally naughty cake is perfect to make as a gift. Look online for great gift wrapping options (see stockists, page 2).

Makes 12
Decorating time:
30 minutes + 1 hour
setting

100 ml (3½ fl oz) **double cream**
75 g (2¾ oz) good quality **dark chocolate**, finely chopped
75 g (2¾ oz) **white chocolate**, finely chopped
75 g (2¾ oz) **unsalted butter**, softened
75 g (2¾ oz) **icing sugar**, sieved
12 **Rich chocolate cupcakes** (see page 6)
15 g (½ oz) shelled **pistachios**, finely chopped
½ x 18 g box **mini marshmallows**
2 x 26 g bars **chocolate coated fudge**, finely sliced

Equipment
disposable piping bag
large star nozzle

Heat the cream in a small saucepan until nearly boiling. Put both the chocolates into a large bowl. Pour over the hot cream and leave to stand for 5 minutes, then gently stir until smooth.

Whisk the butter until fluffy. Gradually add the icing sugar and whisk until combined. Continue whisking, gradually adding all but 2 tablespoons of the chocolate cream, until smooth and fluffy.

Put the chocolate icing into a piping bag with a large star nozzle. Pipe large swirls, starting from the outside edge and working your way to the centre, on top of each cupcake.

Sprinkle each cupcake with a few pistachios, marshmallows and fudge slices. Using the reserved chocolate cream and a teaspoon (or a small piping bag), drizzle a zigzag pattern over the top of each cake. Leave to set for 1 hour.

Pure white cupcakes

These make the perfect cake for a christening celebration. The white doves are available from most good cake shops.

Makes 12
Decorating time:
  30 minutes + setting

150 g (5½ oz) **icing sugar**, sieved, plus extra for dusting
1 teaspoon **unsalted butter**, melted
2–3 tablespoons **boiled water**, cooled
75 g (2¾ oz) **desiccated coconut**
12 **Lime and coconut cupcakes** (see variation, page 6)
100 g (3½ oz) **ready-to-roll white fondant icing**
white mimosa balls
6 **white plastic doves** (optional)
edible cream or lemon glitter

Equipment
flower cutters

Put the icing sugar and butter into a bowl and stir in the water until you get a smooth, thick, but runny, icing. Put the coconut into another bowl. Dip the top of each cupcake into the icing, allow the excess to drip off and then dip into the coconut, gently pressing down until the top of the cupcake is coated.

Lightly dust a clean work surface with a little icing sugar. Roll out the fondant icing until about 3–4 mm (⅛–¼ inch) thick. Cut out a range of large and small flowers using a flower cutter. Press a mimosa ball into the centre of each flower.

Using the leftover runny icing, dab a small amount on to the base of each flower and stick the flowers to the top of the cupcakes. Do the same with the white doves (if using). Sprinkle with a little glitter and leave to set.

New baby cupcakes

Depending on whether the new arrival is a girl or a boy, choose decorations in pink or blue.

Makes 12
Preparation time:
 30 minutes

1 quantity **Lemon buttercream** (see variation, page 10)
12 **Zesty lemon cupcakes** (see page 6)
6 ready-made **blue** or **pink feet sugar decorations**
9 ready-made **blue** or **pink baby sugar decorations**
edible silver balls
edible cream or lemon glitter

Equipment
disposable piping bag
small star nozzle

Spread a little of the buttercream over the tops of six cupcakes using a small palette knife.

Put the remaining buttercream into a piping bag with a small star nozzle and pipe a star border around the edge of the six iced cupcakes. Decorate the remaining cupcakes with small rosettes, starting on the outside edge and working your way into the centre to cover the tops.

Decorate each cupcake with a baby decoration or pair of feet. Sprinkle the piped cupcakes with silver balls and all the cakes a dusting of glitter.

Heart cupcakes

For those romantic moments, these cakes will soon melt any heart.

Makes 12
Decorating time:
30 minutes

1 tablespoon **rose water**
red food colouring
1 quantity **Buttercream** (see page 10)
12 **Zesty lemon cupcakes** (see page 6)
icing sugar, for dusting
75 g (2¾ oz) **ready-to-roll red fondant icing**
red, **heart-shaped sugar sprinkles**
edible red glitter

Equipment
disposable piping bag
large star nozzle
heart-shaped cutter

Mix the rose water and a little red food colouring into the buttercream until the buttercream is pink in colour. Put into a piping bag with a large star nozzle.

Pipe stars over the top of six cupcakes, starting on the outside edge and working your way into the centre to cover the tops. Pipe a big swirl on to the top of the remaining cupcakes, starting on the outside and working your way to the centre.

Lightly dust a clean work surface with icing sugar and roll the fondant icing out until about 3–4 mm (⅛–¼ inch) thick. Using a heart-shaped cookie cutter, stamp out six large hearts.

Decorate the cupcakes with the piped stars with a fondant heart, and scatter the remaining cupcakes with heart-shaped sprinkles. Lightly dust all the cupcakes with a little glitter.

St Patrick's Day cupcakes

With the luck of the Irish, spread the joy with these leprechaun-inspired cakes.

Makes 12
Decorating time:
   30 minutes + 1 hour setting

1 quantity **Buttercream** (see page 10)
green food colouring
12 **Cinnamon cupcakes** (see Dotty name cupcakes, page 24)
4 teaspoons **cold water**
150 g (5½ oz) **royal icing sugar**, sieved
edible silver balls
edible green glitter

Equipment
disposable piping bags
small star nozzle
large petal nozzle

Divide the buttercream in half. Colour one half green using a few drops of green food colouring and beating with a spatula until you get the right shade. Using a small palette knife, spread the green buttercream over the tops of six cupcakes until covered. Cover the remaining cupcakes with the plain buttercream.

Whisk the cold water and icing sugar for a few minutes until stiff peaks form. If it is a little too stiff, add a drop more water. Divide in half. Colour one half green using a few drops of green food colouring and beating with a spatula until you get the right shade.

Put the white icing into a piping bag with a small star nozzle and pipe small stars around the edge of the six cupcakes covered with green buttercream. Put a silver ball on top of each star.

Put the green icing into a piping bag with a large petal nozzle and pipe shamrock petals on top of the remaining cupcakes. Put the leftover icing into another disposable piping bag and snip off the end. Pipe a small stalk on each shamrock. Sprinkle all the cupcakes with glitter and leave to set for 1 hour.

Valentine's Day cupcakes

Let these cupcakes speak from your heart. Be as creative as you like and say as little or as much as you desire.

Makes 12
Preparation and decorating time:
45 minutes + 1 hour setting + cooling
Cooking time:
18–20 minutes

Turkish delight cupcakes
175 g (6 oz) **unsalted butter**, softened
100 g (3½ oz) **caster sugar**
3 **eggs**
175 g (6 oz) **self-raising flour**, sieved
½ teaspoon **baking powder**
1 tablespoon **rose water**
100 g (3½ oz) **rose Turkish delight**, finely diced

To decorate
25 g (1 oz) **unsalted butter**, softened
50 g (1¾ oz) **icing sugar**
1–2 teaspoons **boiled water**, cooled
1 quantity **Chocolate ganache** (see page 13)

Equipment
disposable piping bag
plain writing nozzle

Preheat the oven to 190°C/375°F/Gas Mark 5. Line a 12-hole muffin tin with paper muffin cases.

Whisk the butter and sugar together with an electric hand whisk or beat with a wooden spoon until pale and creamy. Gradually whisk in the eggs until just combined, then add the flour, baking powder and rose water and whisk until combined and fluffy. Fold through the Turkish delight.

Divide the mixture evenly between the paper cases and bake in the oven for 18–20 minutes until golden and risen. Leave to cool in the tin for 5 minutes, then transfer to a wire rack to go cold.

To decorate, whisk the butter until fluffy then gradually sieve in the icing sugar and whisk until it comes together. Add the water and whisk again until light and fluffy.

Using a small palette knife, spread a little of the chocolate ganache over the tops of the cupcakes to cover. Leave to set for 30 minutes.

Put the buttercream into a piping bag with a writing nozzle. Pipe words such as 'I Love You' or 'Be Mine', dots, kisses and heart shapes over the top of the cakes. Leave to set.

Variation Replace the rose Turkish delight with lemon Turkish delight and use 1 tablespoon of lemon juice instead of the rose water.

Mother's Day cupcakes

Say it with flowers this Mother's Day, but instead of a bunch of flowers why not give a bunch of cakes.

Makes 12
Decorating time:
   30 minutes

1 quantity **Orange
   buttercream** (see
   variation, page 10)
pink food colouring
12 **Zesty orange cupcakes**
   (see variation, page 6)
12 ready-made **edible large
   pink flowers**

Equipment
disposable piping bags
large star nozzle
large writing nozzle

Put 3 tablespoons of buttercream into a bowl and mix in a little pink food colouring until light pink in colour.

Using a small palette knife, spread a little of the uncoloured buttercream over the tops of six cupcakes until covered. Put the remaining buttercream into a piping bag with a large star nozzle and pipe a big swirl on to the top of the remaining cupcakes, starting on the outside and working your way to the centre.

Put the pink buttercream into a piping bag with a large writing nozzle. Pipe polka dots over the top of three flat-iced cupcakes, then pipe dots around the edge of the remaining three flat-iced cupcakes. Decorate all the cupcakes with a large pink flower.

St George's Day cupcakes

Raise the flag on 23rd April with these inspired cakes.

Makes 12
Decorating time:
  30 minutes

icing sugar, for dusting
75 g (2¾ oz) **ready-to-roll white fondant icing**
25 g (1 oz) **ready-to-roll red fondant icing**
blue food colouring
1 quantity **Vanilla buttercream** (see variation, page 10)
12 **Truly vanilla cupcakes** (see page 7)
red and blue sugar sprinkles or **confetti**
edible blue glitter

Equipment
4 cm (1½ inch) round cutter

Lightly dust a clean work surface with icing sugar and roll the white fondant icing out until about 5 mm (¼ inch) thick. Using a 4 cm (1½ inch) round cookie cutter, stamp out 12 circles. You may need to re-roll the icing.

Roll a little of the red fondant icing between your fingers and the work surface to make a thin sausage. Cut in half and lay in a cross over the top of one white circle. Lightly roll with a rolling pin to flatten. Re-stamp out the circle and set aside. Repeat with the remaining red fondant icing and white circles to make 12 round St George's flags.

Mix a little blue food colouring into the buttercream until combined and light blue in colour. Using a small palette knife, spread the buttercream over the tops of the cupcakes to cover.

Put a St George's flag on top of each cupcake, pressing down lightly, and then sprinkle the exposed buttercream with the red and blue sprinkles or confetti and a little blue glitter.

Easter nest cupcakes

During the Easter holidays there are lots of different sweets around, so why not use chocolate bunnies or chicks.

Makes 12
Decorating time:
30 minutes + 1 hour setting

150 g (5½ oz) **dark chocolate**, broken into pieces
1 tablespoon **unsalted butter**, softened
25 ml (1 fl oz) **double cream**
25 g (1 oz) **icing sugar**, sieved
2 teaspoons **boiling water**
4 whole **shredded wheat**, crushed
12 **Rich chocolate cupcakes** (see page 6)
about 36 **chocolate mini eggs**

Put the chocolate, butter and double cream in a heatproof bowl and place over a pan of barely simmering water. Gently heat, stirring occasionally until melted.

Stir in the icing sugar until combined. Then stir in the boiling water until you have a smooth icing.

Add the crushed shredded wheat to the bowl and stir with a spatula until coated in the chocolate.

Put a generous spoonful of the topping on top of each cupcake, making a dent in the middle, to make it look like a nest. Arrange the mini eggs in the centre of each nest and leave to set for 1 hour.

Father's Day cupcakes

Make his day special this year and give him a golf course!

Makes 12
Decorating time:
  45 minutes + 1 hour setting

12 **Lime and coconut cupcakes** (see variation, page 6)
75 g (2¾ oz) **unsalted butter**, softened
300 g (10½ oz) **icing sugar**, sieved
juice of 1 **lime**
green food colouring
yellow food colouring
yellow coloured sugar or **yellow sugar strands** or **sprinkles**
non-edible mini golfer figurines
white mimosa balls
cocktail sticks for flag poles

Equipment
disposable piping bags
grass nozzle

Arrange the cupcakes on a serving plate. Whisk the butter until fluffy, then gradually add half the icing sugar and half the lime juice, whisking again until light and fluffy.

Divide the buttercream in half. Colour one half grass green using a few drops of green and yellow food colouring and beating with a spatula until you get the right shade. Colour the remainder a sandy yellow using yellow food colouring.

Put the green buttercream into a piping bag with a grass nozzle and pipe grass-like tufts over some of the cupcakes, creating the outside edge of the golf course.

Using a small palette knife, spread the yellow buttercream over some of the tops of the cupcakes to look like bunkers. Sprinkle generously with the yellow sugar or sprinkles.

Put the remaining icing sugar in a bowl and gradually stir in the remaining lime juice until you get a smooth thick icing. If it is too thick, add a drop more water. Colour with green food colouring until you get a grass-like colour. Put in a disposable piping bag, snip off the end and use to cover any remaining cake, so it looks like a fairway. Leave for 15 minutes until nearly set.

When almost set, arrange the mini golfers on top of the cakes, using the mimosa balls as golf balls. Make a small paper flag and attach to a cocktail stick as a flag pole. Leave for 1 hour to set.

Tip If you can't find coloured sugar, put some granulated sugar in a freezer bag with a little edible yellow dust. Shake to colour the sugar.

Easter egg cupcakes

Forget chocolate eggs this Easter, and make cakes that look like pretty Easter eggs. Use any colours. It's up to you!

Makes 12
Decorating time:
   30 minutes + 1 hour setting

1 quantity **Runny fondant icing** (see page 13)
pink or **red food colouring**
blue food colouring
12 **Turkish delight cupcakes** (see Valentine's Day cupcakes, page 44)

Equipment
disposable piping bag
plain nozzle
cocktail stick

Reserving about 3 tablespoons of icing, divide the remainder into three and put in separate bowls. Colour one-third pink using a few drops of red food colouring and beating with a spatula until you get the right shade. Colour another third pale blue and the last third light purple using blue and pink food colouring. Put the reserved uncoloured icing into a piping bag with a plain nozzle.

Spoon a little of the pink icing over one cupcake, allowing the icing to run over the top to cover it completely. Then, using the piping bag, pipe zigzag lines, spirals or other designs over the top to make it look like a pretty Easter egg. Use a cocktail stick to feather the icing by drawing it across the zigzag lines. Repeat with the remaining cupcakes and icings. Leave to set.

Bonfire Night cupcakes

You can use mint Matchmakers instead. They go well with buttercream flavoured with 1–2 teaspoons of peppermint essence.

Makes 12
Decorating time:
30 minutes

red food colouring
yellow food colouring
1 quantity **Orange buttercream** (see variation, page 10)
12 **Rich chocolate cupcakes** (see page 6)
151 g box **orange Matchmakers**
edible gold glitter

Equipment
disposable piping bag
large star nozzle

Mix a little red and yellow food colouring into the buttercream until combined and orange in colour. Put it into a piping bag with a large star nozzle.

Pipe a large swirl on to the centre of each cupcake, starting a little way in from the outside edge of each cake. Break the Matchmakers into short lengths, depending on the height of your swirls, making some longer than others.

Arrange the Matchmakers around the edge of each swirl, pointing inwards and resting them gently on the buttercream to make it look like a bonfire. Sprinkle with gold glitter.

Halloween cupcakes

This is a great one for children. Be as creative as you like. You could do all monster faces – just colour all the buttercream green.

Makes 12
Decorating time:
  30 minutes

1 quantity **Vanilla buttercream** (see variation, page 10)
green food colouring
black food colouring
12 **Spiced cupcakes** (see variation, page 8)
sweets such as fizzy fangs, liquorice, mini marshmallows, chocolate beans, strawberry pencils and jelly beans
white sugar sprinkles or **strands**
plastic non-edible Halloween cake decorations
edible black glitter

Divide the buttercream in half. Colour one half green using a few drops of green food colouring and beating with a spatula until you get the right shade. Colour the remainder dark grey using the black food colouring.

Using a small palette knife, spread the green buttercream over the tops of six cupcakes until covered. Do the same with the grey buttercream and the remaining cupcakes.

Using the selection of sweets, make monster faces on the green cupcakes. For eyes, use liquorice rolls or cut marshmallows in half and stick brown chocolate beans on top. Finely slice liquorice twists to look like hair, slice strawberry pencils or use red jelly beans to look like teeth.

Sprinkle the grey cupcakes with white sugar sprinkles and top each with a plastic cake decoration and a little black glitter.

Pumpkin cupcakes

Why not use 150 g (5½ oz) of peeled and grated butternut squash or pumpkin instead of the grated carrot?

Makes 12
Decorating time:
  30 minutes

1 quantity **Orange buttercream** (see variation, page 10)
orange food colouring
12 **Carrot cupcakes** (see page 7)
orange sugar sprinkles or **strands**
small nugget **green ready-to-roll fondant icing**

Equipment
disposable piping bag
plain writing nozzle

Colour the buttercream bright orange using the orange food colouring, beating with a spatula until you get the right shade.

Reserve about 3 tablespoons of buttercream. Using a small palette knife, spread the remaining buttercream over the tops of the cupcakes until covered.

Put a cupcake on a plate and sprinkle liberally with the orange sugar strands until completely covered. The plate should catch the excess sugar strands. Scoop these up each time and use on the next cupcake. Repeat so all the cupcakes are covered.

Put the reserved buttercream into a piping bag with a plain writing nozzle. Pipe a line around the edge of each cupcake, one across the centre and then two slightly curved lines to either side of the central line, all starting and ending at the same point so they look like the segments of a pumpkin.

Make small stalks using the green fondant icing, shaping them into short triangles. Arrange at the top of each cupcake where the lines meet.

Christmas bauble cupcakes

Make these cakes really Christmassy with cranberries. Omit the poppy seeds and use 50 g (1¾ oz) of dried cranberries instead.

Makes 12
Decorating time:
30 minutes + 1 hour setting

icing sugar, for dusting
100 g (3½ oz) **ready-to-roll white fondant icing**
12 **Poppy seed cupcakes** (see variation, page 6)
50 g (1¾ oz) **apricot jam**, melted
100 g (3½ oz) **ready-to-roll red fondant icing**
100 g (3½ oz) **ready-to-roll green fondant icing**
4 teaspoons **cold water**
150 g (5½ oz) **royal icing sugar**, sieved
edible silver and **gold balls**

Equipment
6.5 cm (2½ inch) round cutter
disposable piping bag
plain writing nozzle

Lightly dust a clean work surface with a little icing sugar. Roll out the white fondant icing until about 3–4 mm (⅛–¼ inch) thick. Then, using a 6.5 cm (2½ inch) round cookie cutter, stamp out four circles. You may need to re-roll the icing.

Brush the tops of four cupcakes with the apricot jam then put a white circle on each, lightly pressing down. Repeat with the red and green fondant icing and the remaining cupcakes.

Whisk the cold water and icing sugar together for a few minutes until stiff peaks form. If it is a little too stiff, add a drop more water. Put into a piping bag with a plain writing nozzle.

Pipe a circle around the outside edge of each cupcake and then pipe curved lines, dots, zigzags or stars in the centre of each cupcake to look like a bauble. Decorate with gold or silver balls. Leave to set for 1 hour.

Christmas wreath cupcakes

Why not give cakes this Christmas? Look for cupcake boxes or online for great gift wrapping options (see stockists, page 2).

Makes 12
Preparation and
  decorating time:
  40 minutes + 1 hour
  setting + cooling
Cooking time:
  18–20 minutes

125 g (4½ oz) **unsalted butter**, softened
175 g (6 oz) **caster sugar**
3 **eggs**
175 g (6 oz) **self-raising flour**, sieved
150 g (5½ oz) **luxury mincemeat**

To decorate
icing sugar, for dusting
250 g (9 oz) **ready-to-roll white fondant icing**
50 g (1¾ oz) **apricot jam**, melted
300 g (10½ oz) **royal icing sugar**
green food colouring
red sugar balls

Equipment
5.5 cm (2¼ inch) round cutter
disposable piping bag
small leaf nozzle

Preheat the oven to 190°C/375°F/Gas Mark 5. Line a 12-hole muffin tin with paper muffin cases.

Whisk the butter and sugar together with an electric hand whisk or beat with a wooden spoon until pale and creamy. Gradually whisk in the eggs until just combined. Add the flour and mincemeat and whisk again until combined and fluffy.

Divide between the paper cases and bake in the oven for 18–20 minutes until golden and risen. Leave to cool in the tin for 5 minutes, then transfer to a wire rack to go cold.

Lightly dust a clean work surface with a little icing sugar. Roll out the fondant icing until about 3–4 mm (⅛–¼ inch) thick. Then, using a 5.5 cm (2¼ inch) round cookie cutter, stamp out 12 circles. You may need to re-roll the icing. Brush the tops of the cupcakes with the apricot jam then put a white circle on each, lightly pressing down.

Whisk the royal icing sugar and 2 tablespoons cold water together for 5 minutes until stiff peaks form. Add a little green food colouring and continue to whisk until you have the right colour.

Put the icing into a piping bag with a leaf nozzle. Working all the way around the outside edge of each cupcake, pipe in a zigzag motion, slightly overlapping the fondant icing. Decorate with red sugar balls and leave to set for 1 hour.

Fruit tart cupcakes

You can top these cupcakes with any fruits you like, such as fresh apricots or figs, or vary them depending on the season.

Makes 12
**Preparation and
   decorating time:
   30 minutes + cooling**
**Cooking time:
   15–18 minutes**

125 g (4½ oz) **unsalted
   butter**, softened
125 g (4½ oz) **caster sugar**
2 **eggs**
125 g (4½ oz) **self-raising
   flour**
2 **kiwi fruit**, peeled and cut
   into 12 slices
12 **green** or **red seedless
   grapes**
6 **strawberries**, sliced

Crème patisserie
4 **egg yolks**
60 g (2 oz) **caster sugar**
2 teaspoons **cornflour**
25 g (1 oz) **plain flour**
1 teaspoon **vanilla extract**
300 ml (10 fl oz) **milk**

Preheat the oven to 190°C/375°F/Gas Mark 5. Line a 12-hole muffin tin with paper muffin cases.

Whisk the butter and sugar together with an electric hand whisk or beat with a wooden spoon until pale and creamy. Gradually whisk in the eggs until just combined. Add the self-raising flour and whisk again until combined and fluffy.

Divide between the paper cases and bake in the oven for 15–18 minutes until golden and risen. Leave to cool in the tin for 5 minutes, then transfer to a wire rack to go cold.

Meanwhile, for the crème patisserie, mix together the egg yolks, sugar, cornflour, plain flour and vanilla extract. Put the milk in a small pan and bring just to the boil. Gradually stir into the egg yolk mixture until smooth and combined. Rinse out the pan and return the hot milk mixture. Gently bring to the boil, stirring until thickened. Transfer to a bowl, cover with a damp piece of greaseproof paper and leave to go cold.

When the crème patisserie and cakes are cold, whisk the crème patisserie with a fork to loosen and then spoon a little on to the top of each cupcake, levelling the top with a small palette knife.

Arrange the fruit on top of each cake and serve immediately or store in the fridge until required.

New Year cupcakes

When the clock strikes 12, indulge in a clock-inspired cupcake. Arrange like a clock on a serving platter.

Makes 12
Decorating time:
  30 minutes

1 quantity **Coffee buttercream** (see variation, page 10)
12 **Coffee and almond cupcakes** (see page 8)
icing sugar, for dusting
100 g (3½ oz) **ready-to-roll black fondant icing**
edible gold glitter

Equipment
disposable piping bag
large shell nozzle
large number cutters

Put the buttercream into a piping bag with a large shell nozzle and pipe a continuous line all the way around the edge of a cupcake. Then pipe small rosettes all over the centre of the cake until the top of the cake is covered. Repeat with the remaining cupcakes.

Lightly dust a clean work surface with a little icing sugar. Roll out the black fondant icing until about 3–4 mm (⅛–¼ inch) thick. Using large number cookie cutters stamp out the numbers 1 to 12.

Sprinkle the tops of the cupcakes with a little gold glitter. Top each cake with a number from 1–12 and arrange in a circle like a clock.

Tip If you like you could make paper clock hands out of black card and put them in the middle of the arranged cupcakes.

Vintage chic cupcakes

If you wish, keep the cupcakes in their cases and just decorate the tops using 300 g (10½ oz) of ready-to-roll fondant icing.

Makes 12
Decorating time: 1 hour
+ 1 hour setting

900 g (2 lb) **ready-to-roll ivory fondant icing**
pink food colouring
blue food colouring
green food colouring
12 **Zesty lemon cupcakes** (see page 6)
100 g (3½ oz) **apricot jam**, melted
icing sugar, for dusting
boiled water, cooled
150 g (5½ oz) **royal icing sugar**, sieved
4 teaspoons **cold water**
ready-made **sugar flowers**

Equipment
5 cm (2 inch) round cutter
disposable piping bag
plain writing nozzle

Divide the fondant icing into three equal pieces. Wrap each piece in cling film while you work to prevent it from drying out. Colour one piece pale pink using the pink food colouring. Colour a second piece pale turquoise using a little blue and green food colouring.

Take a cupcake out of its paper case and discard the case. Brush the cake all over the top and sides with apricot jam and place on a board.

Lightly dust a clean work surface with a little icing sugar. Roll a quarter of the ivory fondant icing out until about 3 mm (⅛ inch) thick. Cut out a 20 x 4 cm (8 x 1½ inch) rectangle. Wrap the rectangle around the sides of the cupcake, smoothing with your hands to cover the sides of the cake and just overlapping the top.

Reroll the trimmings and stamp out a circle using a 5 cm (2 inch) round cutter. Brush the rim with a little cooled water and place on top of the cake, pressing down gently and reshaping where necessary. Repeat with the remaining cupcakes and icings. You should end up with four ivory, four pink and four turquoise cupcakes.

Whisk the icing sugar and cooled water for a few minutes until stiff peaks form. If it is a little too stiff, add a drop more water. Put the icing into a piping bag with a plain writing nozzle.

Pipe different designs on each cupcake, such as small dots around the edge, lines across the middle or swirls over the top and sides. Finish each with a sugar flower. Arrange on a serving plate and leave to set for 1 hour.

Tips Do not store in an airtight container, as the icing will become sweaty. The cakes will stay fresh for at least 3 days once iced.

To finish the look, why not tie a ribbon around the middle of each cake and secure with a little royal icing.

Spring blossom cupcakes

You can find a range of flower cutters from most good cake shops, including gerberas, daisies and marguerites.

Makes 12
Decorating time:
  30 minutes

1 quantity **Lemon buttercream** (see variation, page 10)
blue food colouring
12 **Raspberry swirl cupcakes** (see variation, page 7)
icing sugar, for dusting
125 g (4½ oz) **ready-to-roll white fondant icing**
edible silver balls

Equipment
flower cutters
disposable piping bag
writing nozzle

Reserve 2 tablespoons of the buttercream. Colour the remaining buttercream with a few drops of blue food colouring, beating with a spatula until light blue. Spread the blue buttercream over the tops of the cupcakes using a small palette knife.

Lightly dust a clean work surface with icing sugar and roll the fondant icing out until about 3–4 mm (⅛–¼ inch) thick. Using a selection of large, medium and small flower cutters, stamp out lots of flowers until the icing has been used up. Arrange a few different sized flowers on top of each cupcake, spacing them so they look like spring blossom.

Put the reserved buttercream into a piping bag with a plain writing nozzle and pipe flower stems joining some of the flowers together and coming from the side of each cake.

Prick a hole in the centre of any large flowers using a skewer. Arrange a silver ball in the centre of each flower.

Tip If making for a wedding, this recipe can easily be doubled depending on how many cupcakes you need. The cupcakes with the blue butter cream on them can also be frozen in advance. Just defrost and decorate with the flowers, stems and silver balls.

Chocolate dream cupcakes

Depending on the number of guests, why not make batches of cakes and freeze them. Then all that's left is to defrost and ice.

Makes 12
Decorating time:
 30 minutes

icing sugar, for dusting
150 g (5½ oz) **ready-to-roll chocolate fondant icing**
12 **Rich chocolate cupcakes** (see page 6)
25 g (1 oz) **apricot jam**, melted
1 quantity **Chocolate buttercream** (see variation, page 10)
edible gold glitter
ready-made **chocolate decorations** or **flowers**

Equipment
6.5 cm (2½ inch) round cutter
disposable piping bags
medium star nozzle

Lightly dust a clean work surface with a little icing sugar. Roll out the fondant icing until about 3–4 mm (⅛–¼ inch) thick. Then, using a 6.5 cm (2½ inch) round cookie cutter, stamp out six circles. You may need to re-roll the icing.

Brush the tops of six cupcakes with the apricot jam then put a circle on the top of each cupcake, lightly pressing down.

Put the buttercream into a piping bag with a medium star nozzle and pipe small stars around the edge of the iced cupcakes. Pipe stars around the edge of the remaining cupcakes. Finish with a swirl in the centre of these cupcakes.

Transfer the leftover buttercream into a disposable piping bag and snip a tiny piece off the end. Pipe four lines across the centre of four fondant iced cupcakes, crossing in the centre.

Sprinkle the cupcakes with a little edible glitter and then decorate all but those with the iced lines with a chocolate decoration or flower, using buttercream to stick them down if necessary.

Monogram cupcakes

The fondant hearts can be made in advance and stored between baking parchment. Do not store in an airtight container.

Makes 12
Decorating time:
  30 minutes +
  24 hours drying

icing sugar, for dusting
75 g (3¾ oz) **flower paste**
  (see Tip, page 93)
75 g (3¾ oz) **ready-to-roll**
  white fondant icing
1 quantity **Orange**
  buttercream (see
  variation, page 10)
pink food colouring
blue food colouring
12 **Gorgeous ginger**
  cupcakes (see page 8)

Equipment
medium heart cutter
small alphabet cutters
disposable piping bag's
large star nozzle
small writing nozzle

Lightly dust a clean work surface with a little icing sugar. Mix together the flower paste and fondant icing, then roll out until about 3–4 mm (⅛–¼ inch) thick. Using a medium heart cookie cutter, stamp out 12 hearts. You may need to re-roll the icing. Using small alphabet cookie cutters, lightly press the initials of the bride and groom into the hearts. Set aside and leave to dry for at least 24 hours.

Reserve 2 tablespoons of buttercream. Colour the remaining buttercream pastel purple using a few drops of pink and blue food colouring and beating with a spatula until you get the right shade.

Put the purple buttercream into a disposable piping bag with a large star nozzle and pipe a swirl of buttercream around the edge of each cupcake, lifting the nozzle up when you get to the start.

Snip the end of the piping bag off, just after the nozzle. It should leave about a 2 cm (¾ inch) opening in the piping bag. Pipe a large dollop of buttercream in the centre of each cupcake.

Put the reserved buttercream into a disposable piping bag with a small writing nozzle and pipe over the letters on each heart. When ready to serve, arrange the hearts on top of each cupcake.

Tip For an added touch, put 2 tablespoons of the purple buttercream into a piping bag with a writing nozzle. Pipe small dots around the edge of each heart.

Good luck cupcakes

Wish someone well with these simple yet totally delicious cakes. Silver horseshoes are available from most good cake shops.

Makes 12
Preparation and decorating time:
30 minutes + 1 hour setting
Cooking time:
15–20 minutes

175 g (6 oz) **unsalted butter**, softened
150 g (5½ oz) **caster sugar**
3 **eggs**
175 g (6 oz) **self-raising flour**, sieved
½ teaspoon **baking powder**
2 tablespoons **milk**
½ teaspoon **vanilla extract**
75 g (2¾ oz) **chocolate Bourbon biscuits**, roughly chopped

To decorate
1 quantity **Runny fondant icing** (see page 13)
non-edible silver horseshoes
silver and white sugar balls

Preheat the oven to 200°C/400°F/Gas Mark 6. Line a 12-hole muffin tin with paper muffin cases.

Whisk the butter and sugar together with an electric hand whisk or beat with a wooden spoon until pale and creamy. Gradually whisk in the eggs until just combined. Using a metal spoon, fold in the flour, baking powder, milk, vanilla extract and biscuits until combined.

Divide between the paper cases and bake in the oven for 15–20 minutes until golden and risen. Leave to cool in the tin for 5 minutes, then transfer to a wire rack to go cold.

Spoon a little of the icing over each cupcake, allowing it to run and cover the top of the cakes completely. Put a horseshoe in the centre of each cake and then sprinkle with the silver and white sugar balls. Leave to set for 1 hour.

Lavender cupcakes

You can find dried lavender among the herbs and spices in the supermarkets or buy dried stems from a florist.

Makes 12
Preparation and decorating time:
   30 minutes
Cooking time:
   20 minutes

125 ml (4 fl oz) **milk**
150 g (5½ oz) **caster sugar**
2 teaspoons **dried lavender**
150 g (5½ oz) **unsalted butter**
¼ teaspoon **bicarbonate of soda**
225 g (8 oz) **self-raising flour**
juice of ½ a **lemon**
3 **eggs**, beaten

To decorate
1 quantity **Marshmallow icing** (see page 12)
pink food colouring
blue food colouring
ready-made **purple sugar flowers**
edible crystallised violets

Preheat the oven to 180°C/350°F/Gas Mark 4. Line a 12-hole muffin tin with paper muffin cases.

Put the milk, sugar, lavender and butter in a small pan and gently heat until combined. Stir in the bicarbonate of soda and leave to cool.

Meanwhile, put the flour and lemon juice in a bowl. Add the eggs and stir with a spatula until combined. Gradually stir in the warm milk mixture.

Divide between the paper cases and bake in the oven for 20 minutes until golden and risen. Leave to cool in the tin for 5 minutes, then transfer to a wire rack to go cold.

Colour the marshmallow icing pastel purple using a few drops of pink and blue food colouring, beating with a spatula until you get the right shade.

Put a spoonful of icing on each cupcake, allowing it to run over the top. Leave it to settle for about 10 minutes then decorate with the sugar flowers and crystallised violets.

Shell bouquet cupcakes

For ease when planning, make the cakes in advance and freeze.
Then defrost and ice up to 2 days in advance.

Makes 12
Decorating time:
  30 minutes + 1 hour
  setting

1 quantity **Royal icing** (see
  page 13)
12 **Poppy seed cupcakes**
  (see variation, page 6)
**edible diamond cream
  glitter** or **dust**

Equipment
disposable piping bags
small shell nozzle
small rope nozzle

Using a small palette knife, spread a little of the royal icing over the tops of four cupcakes until covered. Set aside to dry.

Place 2 tablespoons of royal icing in a disposable piping bag and snip a tiny piece off the end. Put half the remaining royal icing into a piping bag with a small shell nozzle and pipe shells on the tops of a further four cupcakes, starting on the outside edge and working your way into the centre.

Using the shell nozzle again, pipe six shells like a flower in the centre of the flat iced cupcakes, piping one final shell in the centre of each flower. Using the reserved icing in the piping bag, pipe small dots in a continuous wavy pattern around the shell flower.

Put the remaining royal icing into a piping bag with a small rope nozzle and pipe medium dots on the tops of the last four cupcakes, starting on the outside edge and working your way into the centre. Let the first layer dry and then go back over the dots and pipe some more to give the cupcakes some height.

Leave all the cupcakes to dry and then sprinkle with edible glitter.

Tip You could colour the royal icing using a little food colouring to match the colour scheme of a party or wedding.

Red rose cupcakes

Use rose petals to match a colour scheme. Chocolate scrolls are available from most good cake shops (see stockists, page 2).

Makes 12
Decorating time:
30 minutes + 1 hour setting

1 quantity **White chocolate ganache** (see variation, page 13)
1 tablespoon **boiling water**
12 **White chocolate chip cupcakes** (see variation, page 6)
ready-made **white chocolate scrolls**, cut in half if large
fresh **red rose petals**

Put the white chocolate ganache in the fridge for 30 minutes until it is firm but not solid. Whisk with an electric hand whisk until light and fluffy, then add the boiling water and whisk again.

Using a small palette knife, spread the chocolate ganache over the tops of the cupcakes until covered.

Decorate each cupcake with three chocolate scrolls and a rose petal. Leave to set for 1 hour.

Tip If you can't find white chocolate scrolls, then you can make your own. Simply melt 100 g (3½ oz) of white chocolate cake covering and spread on to a glass chopping board or piece of marble. Set aside until the chocolate is nearly set then, using a sharp knife, scrape the knife along the chocolate away from you to make curls. Leave to set before using.

Diamond wedding cupcakes

Edible diamonds are available from most good cake shops or online (see stockists, page 2).

Makes 12
Decorating time:
  30 minutes

125 g (4½ oz) **unsalted butter**, softened
250 g (9 oz) **icing sugar**, sieved
1 large ripe **passion fruit**
12 **Zesty lemon cupcakes** (see page 6)
icing sugar, for dusting
50 g (1¾ oz) **ready-to-roll ivory fondant icing**
edible cream glitter
12 **edible sugar diamonds**

Equipment
disposable piping bag
large petal nozzle
2 cm (¾ inch) round cutter
embossing tool or cocktail stick

Whisk the butter until fluffy. Gradually add the icing sugar and whisk until it comes together. Cut the passion fruit in half and pass the juice and seeds through a sieve to remove the seeds. Add the juice to the buttercream and whisk again until light and fluffy.

Put the buttercream into a piping bag with a large petal nozzle and pipe petal shapes over the tops of the cupcakes, starting on the outside edge and working your way into the centre.

Lightly dust a clean work surface with a little icing sugar. Roll out the fondant icing until about 3–4 mm (⅛–¼ inch) thick. Then, using a 2 cm (¾ inch) round cookie cutter, stamp out 12 small circles. Using an embossing tool or skewer, make a small dent in the middle of each circle. Put a circle on top of each cake.

Sprinkle the cakes with the edible glitter. When ready to serve, put an edible diamond on top of each circle, using the dent to hold it in place.

Tip Edible diamonds are extremely susceptible to humidity, so only put them on top of the cakes when ready to serve.

Pearl wedding cupcakes

If you can't find pearlised lustre edible spray, brush the tops all over with edible silver lustre dust or powder.

Makes 12
Decorating time:
  30 minutes + 1 hour setting

icing sugar, for dusting
300 g (10½ oz) **ready-to-roll white fondant icing**
pearlised lustre edible spray
12 **Totally almond cupcakes** (see variation, page 8)
50 g (1¾ oz) **apricot jam,** melted
4 teaspoons **cold water**
150 g (5½ oz) **royal icing sugar,** sieved
edible oyster pearl balls or **dragées**

Equipment
6 cm (2½ inch) crinkled round cutter
disposable piping bag
medium rope nozzle

Lightly dust a clean work surface with a little icing sugar. Roll out the fondant icing until about 3–4 mm (⅛–¼ inch) thick and spray all over with the pearlised spray so it is evenly covered. Leave to dry for a few minutes.

Using a 6 cm (2½ inch) crinkled edge round cookie cutter, stamp out 12 circles. Brush the tops of the cupcakes with the apricot jam then put a circle on the top of each cupcake, lightly pressing down.

Whisk the cold water and icing sugar for a few minutes until stiff peaks form. If it is a little too stiff, add a drop more water; if it is a little too runny, add a little icing sugar.

Put the icing into a piping bag with a medium rope nozzle and pipe medium dots, spaced a little apart, around the outside edge of the fondant circle on six cupcakes. Put a pearl ball on top of each dot. Pipe a continuous loop pattern around the edge of the remaining cupcakes and put a pearl ball into each loop. Leave to set for 1 hour.

Tip You can also spray the cakes with the pearlised spray once the fondant icing has been put on.

Place name cupcakes

Why not add a touch of glamour to the dinner table and impress your friends with these tasty name cards?

Makes 12
Decorating time:
20 minutes

1 quantity **Chocolate glacé icing** (see variation, page 12)
12 **Spiced cupcakes** (see variation, page 8)
multi-coloured sugar sprinkles
cocktail sticks with name cards stuck on

Using a small palette knife, spread a little of the chocolate icing over the cupcakes to cover the tops completely. Leave to settle for 5 minutes then scatter a few sprinkles over the top and leave to set. Finish with the name cards.

Tip This will work just as well with any of the other frostings and icings, especially the chocolate ganache (see page 13).

Passing exams cupcakes

You don't have to use miniature plastic champagne glasses – just cover the cakes in more caramel balls.

Makes 12
Decorating time:
   30 minutes +
   30 minutes cooling

1 quantity **Chocolate buttercream** (see variation, page 10)
12 **Mocha cupcakes** (see variation, page 6)
chocolate-covered caramel balls
3 **non-edible mini champagne glasses** (optional)
½ packet **powdered gelatine** (optional)
75 ml (3 fl oz) **boiling water** (optional)

Using a small palette knife, spread the buttercream over the tops of the cupcakes until covered. Swirl the buttercream with the tip of the palette knife. Scatter the caramel balls over the tops of the cupcakes.

To make the champagne to fill the glasses, dissolve the gelatine in the boiling water and whisk with a hand whisk until frothy. Pour a little into each champagne glass and leave for 30 minutes until set. Place on top of three of the cupcakes.

Ruby wedding cupcakes

Top the cakes with any ruby red sweets or sugar decorations. You could also use red sugar flowers if you liked.

Makes 12
Decorating time:
   30 minutes

icing sugar, for dusting
150 g (5½ oz) **ready-to-roll ivory fondant icing**
12 **Golden syrup cupcakes** (see variation, page 8)
25 g (1 oz) **apricot jam**, melted
100 g (3½ oz) **unsalted butter**, softened
200 g (7 oz) **golden icing sugar**, sieved
1 tablespoon **golden syrup**
edible red glitter
12 **red jelly diamonds**

Equipment
6 cm (2½ inch) crinkled round cutter
disposable piping bag
large star nozzle

Lightly dust a clean work surface with a little icing sugar. Roll out the fondant icing until about 3–4 mm (⅛–¼ inch) thick. Using a 6 cm (2½ inch) crinkled edge round cookie cutter, stamp out six circles. You may need to re-roll the icing.

Brush the tops of six cupcakes with the apricot jam then put a circle on the top of each cupcake, lightly pressing down.

Whisk the butter until fluffy. Gradually add the icing sugar and golden syrup and whisk again until light and fluffy.

Put the buttercream into a piping bag with a large star nozzle and pipe a small star in the centre of the six fondant-iced cupcakes. Pipe a large swirl on the top of the remaining cupcakes, starting from the outside edge and working your way into the centre. Sprinkle these with a little red glitter.

Put a jelly diamond on top of the buttercream on each cupcake to finish.

Strawberry cupcakes

These make the perfect treat to accompany the tennis at Wimbledon! Or they're just the ticket for an afternoon tea.

Makes 12
Preparation and
decorating time:
    45 minutes + cooling
Cooking time:
    18–20 minutes

175 g (6 oz) **unsalted butter**,
   softened
125 g (4½ oz) **caster sugar**
3 **eggs**
175 g (6 oz) **self-raising flour**
½ teaspoon **baking powder**
75 g (2¾ oz) **strawberry jam**

To decorate
1 quantity **Vanilla cream**
   cheese frosting (see
   variation, page 10)
12 fresh **strawberries**

Equipment
disposable piping bag

Preheat the oven to 190°C/375°F/Gas Mark 5. Line a 12-hole muffin tin with paper muffin cases.

Whisk the butter and sugar with an electric hand whisk or beat with a wooden spoon until pale and creamy. Gradually whisk in the eggs until just combined. Add the flour and baking powder and whisk again until combined and fluffy. Fold through the strawberry jam.

Divide between the paper cases and bake in the oven for 18–20 minutes until golden and risen. Leave to cool in the tin for 5 minutes, then transfer to a wire rack to go cold.

Put the cream cheese frosting in a disposable piping bag and snip the end off so it has about a 2 cm (¾ inch) opening. Pipe a large swirl in the centre of each cupcake. Top each swirl with a strawberry. Store in the fridge until required.

Driving test cupcakes

Draw small red 'L' letters (or green 'P' letters) on to white paper, cut out and stick on to cocktail sticks to finish the look.

Makes 12
Decorating time:
30 minutes

100 g (3½ oz) **unsalted butter**, softened
100 g (3½ oz) **dulce de leche**
200 g (7 oz) **icing sugar**, sieved
red food colouring
brown food colouring
12 **Totally nuts cupcakes** (see variation, page 8)
non-edible plastic cars (optional)
non-edible 'L' plate flags (see recipe introduction, optional)

Equipment
disposable piping bag
large star nozzle

Whisk the butter and dulce de leche together until fluffy. Gradually add the icing sugar and whisk again until light and fluffy.

Divide the buttercream into three. Colour one-third pink using a few drops of red food colouring, beating with a spatula until you get the right shade. Colour another third light brown using brown food colouring, beating again with a spatula.

Fill a piping bag that has a large star nozzle with alternating spoonfuls of the three buttercreams and pipe large swirls on top of each cupcake. Decorate each with either a car or a 'L' plate flag.

Spots 'v' stripes cupcakes

You can vary the colours as you wish. If you can't find the one you want, colour ready-to-roll white fondant icing using food colouring.

Makes 12
Decorating time:
   45 minutes

icing sugar, for dusting
275 g (9½ oz) **ready-to-roll white fondant icing**
50 g (1¾ oz) **ready-to-roll blue fondant icing**
12 **Zesty lemon cupcakes** (see page 6)
50 g (1¾ oz) **apricot jam**, melted
50 g (1¾ oz) **ready-to-roll green fondant icing**

Equipment
6.5 cm (2½ inch) round cutter
2.5 cm (1 inch) round cutter
1.5 cm (⅝ inch) round cutter
cocktail stick

For the striped cupcakes, lightly dust a clean work surface with a little icing sugar. Roll out 125 g (4½ oz) of white fondant icing to an 18 cm (7 inch) square about 5 mm (¼ inch) thick. Roll out the blue fondant icing to an 18 x 9 cm (7 x 3½ inch) rectangle of the same thickness.

Cut the white icing into seven and strips space them just slightly apart. Cut the blue icing into six strips and place them between the white strips, so the colours alternate. Press the strips gently together so there are no gaps. Lightly roll with a rolling pin to join the strips together.

Using a 6.5 cm (2½ inch) round cookie cutter, stamp out six circles. Brush the tops of six cupcakes with the apricot jam then put a stripy circle on the top of each, lightly pressing down.

For the spotty cupcakes, lightly dust the work surface again with a little icing sugar. Roll out the remaining white fondant then the green fondant icing until both are about 5 mm (¼ inch) thick.

Using a 2.5 cm (1 inch) and a 1.5 cm (⅝ inch) round cutter, stamp out at least 25 circles randomly from the white icing, leaving small spaces between the circles. Cut out the same number of circles from the green icing, re-rolling this icing if necessary. Reserve the circles.

Remove the white circles from their holes (if necessary) and replace with a green circle. The icing should now be white with green spots. Lightly roll with a rolling pin to join the colours.

Using a 6.5 cm (2½ inch) round cookie cutter, stamp out six circles. Brush the tops of the remaining cupcakes with the apricot jam then put a spotty circle on the top of each, lightly pressing down.

Animal cupcakes

Create your own zoo or farmyard with these great animal cakes.

Makes 12
Decorating time:
  45 minutes

300 g (10½ oz) **ready-to-roll white fondant icing**
pink food colouring
yellow food colouring
75 g (2¾ oz) **unsalted butter**, softened
150 g (5½ oz) **icing sugar**, sieved, plus extra for dusting
1 tablespoon **boiled water**, cooled, plus extra for brushing
12 **Carrot cupcakes** (see page 7)
50 g (1¾ oz) **apricot jam**, melted
ready-made **black writing icing**
brown food colouring

Equipment
7 cm (2¾ inch) round cutter
4 cm (1½ inch) round cutter
cocktail stick
shell and grass nozzles
disposable piping bags

Divide the fondant icing into three pieces. Colour one-third pink using a few drops of pink food colouring. Colour another third yellow using the yellow food colouring. Wrap all the pieces in cling film to prevent them drying out.

Whisk the butter until fluffy. Gradually add the icing sugar and about 1–2 teaspoons of the water and whisk again until light and fluffy. Set aside.

Lightly dust a clean work surface with a little icing sugar. Roll out the white fondant icing until about 3–4 mm (⅛–¼ inch) thick and, using a 7 cm (2¾ inch) round cookie cutter, stamp out four circles. You may need to re-roll the icing.

Brush the tops of four cupcakes with the apricot jam then put a white circle on the top of each cupcake, lightly pressing down. Repeat with the pink and yellow icing and remaining cupcakes. Reserve the leftover icing.

For the pig, re-roll the reserved pink icing and, using a 4 cm (1½ inch) round cookie cutter, stamp out four circles. Brush one side with a little of the water and stick just off centre on each pink cupcake. Place small triangles at the top for the ears and add small, slightly flattened balls for the snout and feet. Use a cocktail stick to make nostrils and toes. Pipe small black eyes with the writing icing and shape any leftover pink icing into a curly tail.

For the sheep, make four small balls, about the size of a Malteser, with some of the reserved white icing. Flatten slightly and stick just off centre on each white cupcake. Put the buttercream into a piping bag with a shell nozzle and pipe small shells all around the head to look like wool. Finish by making floppy ears and feet with the last of the white icing and piping eyes and a mouth using the writing icing. Use a cocktail stick to make toes.

For the lion, make four small balls, about the size of a big Malteser, with some of the reserved yellow icing. Flatten slightly and stick just off centre on each yellow cupcake. Make small balls and flatten slightly for the cheeks. Colour the remaining buttercream with the brown food colouring. Put into a piping bag with a grass nozzle and pipe a mane around the head. Pipe small black eyes and whiskers with the writing icing. Use a cocktail stick to mark the cheeks and toes.

Daisy cupcakes

This simple yet effective design can transform any cupcake. Why not give it a go with other flower shapes?

Makes 12
Decorating time:
  30 minutes

icing sugar, for dusting
150 g (5½ oz) **ready-to-roll white fondant icing**
yellow chocolate beans
1 quantity **Orange cream cheese frosting** (see variation, page 10)
12 **Raspberry swirl cupcakes** (see variation, page 7)
edible yellow glitter

Equipment
daisy flower cutter

Lightly dust a clean work surface with a little icing sugar. Roll out the fondant icing until about 3–4 mm (⅛–¼ inch) thick. Cut out 36 small daisies using a daisy-style flower cutter. You may need to re-roll the icing. Push a chocolate bean into the centre of each flower.

Using a small palette knife, spread the cream cheese frosting over the tops of the cupcakes until covered. Sprinkle the cupcakes with a little edible glitter and then top each with three daisies. Serve immediately or store in the fridge for up to 3 days.

Enchanted cupcakes

Create a fairytale land with these toadstool cakes. Why not top them with non-edible fairy cake toppers or butterflies as well.

Makes 12
Decorating time: 30 minutes + 1 hour setting

50 g (1¾ oz) **ready-to-roll white fondant icing**
15 g (½ oz) **flower paste**
icing sugar, for dusting
12 **Truly vanilla cupcakes** (see page 7)
75 g (2¾ oz) **strawberry jam**
1 quantity **Glacé icing** (see page 12)
red food colouring
70 g (2½ oz) **white chocolate buttons**

Equipment
butterfly cookie cutter

Mix together the fondant icing and the flower paste. Lightly dust a clean work surface with a little icing sugar. Roll out the fondant icing until about 3 mm (⅛ inch) thick. Then, using a small or medium butterfly cutter, stamp out a few butterflies. Make a large 'M' shape from some foil and rest the butterflies in the foil to bend the wings up slightly. Leave to dry for 1 hour.

Meanwhile, using a small, serrated knife, cut a cone shape from the top of each cake. Put a little strawberry jam into the holes and replace the cones.

Colour the glacé icing red with a few drops of red food colouring, beating with a spatula until you get the right shade. If the icing goes too runny you may need to add a little more sieved icing sugar. Put a spoonful of the icing on the top of each cupcake, allowing it to run and cover the top. Leave to set for 5–10 minutes.

Decorate the tops of the cupcakes with chocolate buttons to look like toadstools, cutting some in half and putting them around the edges. Finish with the butterflies and leave to set completely.

Tip Flower paste is a ready-made sugar paste that is ideal for making sugar flowers or other detailed figures, such as butterflies. It is available from cake shops or online (see stockists, page 2).

Flower power cupcakes

You may have to sort through the chocolate beans to pick out the right colours to match your icing.

Makes 12
Decorating time:
30 minutes

1 quantity **Lemon buttercream** (see variation, page 10)
12 **Zesty lemon cupcakes** (see page 6)
edible silver glitter
200 g (7 oz) **ready-to-roll white fondant icing**
red or **pink food colouring**
yellow food colouring
icing sugar, for dusting
pink and **orange chocolate beans** or **mini Smarties**

Equipment
large and small flower cutters
disposable piping bag

Reserving 1 tablespoon of the buttercream, spread the remainder over the tops of the cupcakes using a small palette knife. Sprinkle the tops with the silver glitter.

Divide the fondant icing into three pieces. Colour one-third with red or pink food colouring until bright pink, one-third with yellow food colouring until bright yellow and then the remaining piece with a little red and yellow food colouring until bright orange.

Roll each piece of coloured icing into a fat sausage and then press together and gently twist (like a piece of rope). Lightly dust a clean work surface with a little icing sugar and roll out the twisted icing until about 3–4 mm ($\frac{1}{8}$–$\frac{1}{4}$ inch) thick. The colours should blend together.

Using a large flower cutter, stamp out six large flowers. Using a slightly smaller flower cutter, cut out six smaller flowers. Decorate each cupcake with a flower.

Put the reserved buttercream into a piping bag and snip off the end. Pipe a dot in the centre of each flower and then stick on a chocolate bean to finish the flower.

Football cupcakes

You can find the small football players in most cake shops. Or why not try a toy shop for other small football teams?

Makes 12
Decorating time:
30 minutes

1 quantity **Lemon buttercream** (see variation, page 10)
green food colouring
12 **Zesty lemon cupcakes** (see page 6)
12 **plastic non-edible small football players**
2 **plastic non-edible small football goals**
white mimosa ball

Equipment
disposable piping bags
small star nozzle
plain writing nozzle

Reserve about 2 tablespoons of buttercream. Colour the remaining buttercream grass green using a few drops of green food colouring, beating with a spatula until you get the right shade.

Using a small palette knife, spread some of the green buttercream over the tops of the cupcakes until covered. Arrange the cupcakes on a board in a rectangle, like a football pitch.

Put the remaining green buttercream into a piping bag with a small star nozzle. Pipe small stars around the edge of the cupcake rectangle for a border, only piping on the part of each cupcake that is on the outside.

Put the reserved buttercream into a piping bag with a writing nozzle. Pipe a white line around the inside edge of the star border and dots in the corners and halfway point. Pipe two semi-circles at each end of the rectangle to make it look like a football pitch. Finally pipe a line across the middle of the rectangle, and a small circle in the centre. Decorate the cupcakes with football players and goal posts and a mimosa ball for the football.

Tip If you wish, put candles in the corner points, to look like football posts.

Garden cupcakes

This is definitely one to get the kids involved with.
You can be as creative as you like with the decoration.

Makes 12
Decorating time:
  30 minutes

1 quantity **Coffee
  buttercream** (see
  variation, page 10)
12 **Coffee and almond
  cupcakes** (see page 8)
green food colouring
ready-made **sugar flowers**
  and **animals**, such as
  bumble bees, ladybirds,
  rabbits and frogs
sugar butterfly sprinkles

Equipment
disposable piping bag
grass nozzle

Using a small palette knife, spread a little of the buttercream over the tops of the cupcakes until just covered. Colour the remaining buttercream grass green using a few drops of green food colouring, beating with a spatula until you get the right shade.

Put the green buttercream into a piping bag with a grass nozzle. Pipe grass-like tufts all over the tops of the cupcakes, leaving a little of the original coffee-coloured buttercream exposed to look like soil.

Arrange the sugar animals and flowers on top and sprinkle with the butterflies as desired.

Tip If your children don't like coffee, try these using Rich chocolate cupcakes (page 6) with Chocolate buttercream (see variation, page 10).

Fancy button cupcakes

You can make these buttons any colours you like, just use different food colouring or ready-to-roll icing.

Makes 12
Decorating time:
 30 minutes

300 g (10½ oz) **ready-to-roll white fondant icing**
red food colouring
icing sugar, for dusting
50 g (1¾ oz) **seedless raspberry jam**, melted
12 **Zesty orange cupcakes** (see variation, page 6)
ready-made **chocolate or caramel writing icing**

Equipment
6.5 cm (2½ inch) round cutter
4.5 cm (1¾ inch) round cutter
embossing tool or cocktail stick

Colour the fondant icing light pink using a little of the red food colouring, kneading the icing until the correct colour is achieved.

Lightly dust a clean work surface with a little icing sugar. Roll out the fondant icing until about 3–4 mm (⅛–¼ inch) thick. Using a 6.5 cm (2½ inch) round cookie cutter, stamp out 12 circles. You may need to re-roll the icing. Brush the tops of the cupcakes with the raspberry jam then put a pink circle on the top of each, lightly pressing down.

Turn a 4.5 cm (1¾ inch) round cookie cutter upside down so you are using the blunt edge and gently press into the top of each pink circle, to make a circular indentation. Then, using an embossing tool or a cocktail stick, press four holes into the centre of each circle to make it look like a button. If you like you can also press designs into the edge of each button using a star-shaped embossing tool.

Finally, using the writing icing, pipe small lines either diagonally or horizontally between the four holes on each button to look like sewing thread.

Pudding cupcakes

These make a great pudding. They also freeze really well, so make a batch and freeze the un-iced leftovers.

Makes 12
Preparation and
**   decorating time:**
**   25 minutes + cooling**
Cooking time:
**   20–25 minutes**

150 g (5½ oz) fresh
    raspberries
125 g (4½ oz) **unsalted**
    butter, softened
175 g (6 oz) **caster sugar**
1 teaspoon **vanilla extract**
3 **eggs**
125 g (4½ oz) **self-raising**
    flour
200 g (7 oz) **full fat cream**
    cheese

To decorate
300 ml (10 fl oz) **double**
    cream
2 tablespoons **icing sugar**,
    sieved
edible red glitter

Equipment
disposable piping bag
large star nozzle

Preheat the oven to 190°C/375°F/Gas Mark 5. Line a 12-hole muffin tin with paper muffin cases and reserve 12 raspberries to decorate.

Whisk the butter, 125 g (4½ oz) of sugar and vanilla extract together with an electric hand whisk or beat with a wooden spoon until pale and creamy. Gradually whisk in 2 eggs until just combined. Add the flour, whisking again until combined and fluffy.

Whisk the cream cheese and remaining sugar together until combined, then add the remaining egg and continue to whisk until smooth. Pour this mixture into the flour mix, along with the remaining raspberries, and fold together until nearly combined. The mixture will still be quite lumpy.

Divide between the paper cases and bake in the oven for 20–25 minutes until golden and risen. Leave to cool in the tin for 5 minutes, then transfer to a wire rack to go cold.

Whisk the double cream in a bowl until soft peaks form. Stir in the icing sugar to taste. Put the cream into a piping bag with a large star nozzle and pipe a large swirl in the centre of each cupcake. Decorate each with a reserved raspberry and sprinkle with the glitter. Serve immediately or store in the fridge for up to 3 days.

Sweet shop cupcakes

Everyone loves a quarter of sweets. So why not turn your cupcakes into little sweet pots. Use whatever sweets you like.

Makes 12
Decorating time:
  20 minutes

1 quantity **Buttercream** (see page 10)
12 **Golden syrup cupcakes** (see variation, page 8)
red, white and pink sprinkles
retro style sweets, such as foam shrimps, jelly fried eggs, cola bottles and white chocolate mice

Equipment
disposable piping bag

Put the buttercream into a piping bag and snip a piece off the end so it leaves about a 2 cm (¾ inch) opening.

Pipe large swirls on top of each cupcake, starting on the outside and working your way into the centre. Scatter with the red, white and pink sprinkles.

Arrange two sweets in the centre of each cupcake to finish.

Sparkly cupcakes

Once you have discovered edible glitters you won't go back!
Choose your favourite colours to decorate these cakes.

Makes 12
Preparation and
decorating time:
30 minutes + cooling
Cooking time:
20–22 minutes

125 g (4½ oz) **unsalted**
butter, softened
200 g (7 oz) **caster sugar**
3 **eggs**
100 ml (3½ fl oz) **double**
cream
175 g (5½ oz) **self-raising**
flour
75 g (2¾ oz) fresh **raspberries**
75 g (2¾ oz) fresh
blueberries

To decorate
1 quantity **Orange**
buttercream (see
variation, page 10)
edible glitter
edible glitter stars

Equipment
disposable piping bag
large star nozzle

Preheat the oven to 190°C/375°F/Gas Mark 5.
Line a 12-hole muffin tin with paper muffin
cases.

Whisk the butter and sugar together with an
electric hand whisk or beat with a wooden
spoon until pale and creamy. Gradually
whisk in the eggs and cream until just
combined. Then add the flour, whisking again
until combined and fluffy. Fold through the
raspberries and blueberries.

Divide between the paper cases and bake in
the oven for 20–22 minutes until golden and
risen. Leave to cool in the tin for 5 minutes,
then transfer to a wire rack to go cold.

Put the buttercream into a piping bag with
a large star nozzle. Pipe large swirls on top
of each cake, starting from the outside and
working your way into the centre. Sprinkle the
cakes liberally with the glitter and stars.

Ice cream cone cupcakes

These look just like the real thing but won't melt in minutes!

Makes 12
Preparation and
decoration time:
  45 minutes + cooling
Cooking time:
  20–25 minutes

12 **wafer cup cornets**
125 g (4½ oz) **unsalted**
  butter, softened
125 g (4½ oz) **caster sugar**
1 **vanilla pod**, cut in half and
  seeds reserved
2 **eggs**
125 g (4½ oz) **self-raising**
  flour
3 tablespoons **milk**

To decorate
1 quantity **Buttercream** (see
  page 10)
multi-coloured sugar
  strands
4 **Flake bars**, each cut into
  3 lengths

Equipment
disposable piping bag
large star nozzle

Preheat the oven to 190°C/375°F/Gas Mark 5. Stand the cornets in a 12-hole muffin tin – one in each muffin hole.

Whisk the butter, sugar and vanilla seeds together using an electric hand whisk or beat with a wooden spoon until pale and creamy. Gradually whisk in the eggs until just combined. Add the flour and milk and whisk again until combined and fluffy.

Divide between the cornets and bake in the oven for 20–25 minutes until golden and risen. Leave to cool in the tin for 5 minutes, then transfer to a wire rack to go cold.

Put the buttercream into a piping bag with a large star nozzle. Pipe a large swirl, just like a Mr Whippy, on to the top of each cupcake. Scatter over the sugar strands and finish each with a piece of Flake.

Tip To make it easier to fill the cornets, put the cake mixture into a disposable piping bag and snip off the end. Then pipe the mixture evenly into each cornet.

Snowflake cupcakes

You could use other Christmas shapes such as trees. Just use different cutters and red, white and green sprinkles.

Makes 12
Decorating time:
30 minutes + 1 hour setting

1 quantity **Royal icing** (see page 13)
red food colouring
icing sugar, for dusting
75 g (2¾ oz) **ready-to-roll white fondant icing**
12 **Courgette and chocolate cupcakes** (see variation, page 7)
edible sugar snowflake sprinkles

Equipment
large snowflake cutter
disposable piping bag
large star nozzle

Colour the royal icing red with a few drops of red food colouring, beating with a spatula until you get the right shade. If the icing goes too runny you may need to add a little more sieved icing sugar.

Lightly dust a clean work surface with a little icing sugar. Roll out the fondant icing until about 3 mm (⅛ inch) thick then, using a large snowflake cutter, stamp out six snowflakes.

Put the royal icing into a piping bag with a large star nozzle and pipe a large swirl on top of each cupcake, starting from the outside and working your way into the centre. Leave to dry for about 5 minutes.

Sprinkle six cupcakes with the snowflake sprinkles. Arrange the six large snowflakes on top of the remaining cupcakes. Leave to set for 1 hour.

Under the sea cupcakes

You can find lots of different jelly and fizzy sweets in the supermarkets that are in the shape of sea creatures.

Makes 12
Decorating time:
  30 minutes

1 quantity **Vanilla buttercream** (see variation, page 10)
blue food colouring
12 **Marbled chocolate cupcakes** (see variation, page 7)
25 g (1 oz) **ready-to-roll white fondant icing**
black food colouring
fish or **seaside jelly sweets**

Divide the buttercream between two separate bowls. Colour one half sea blue using a few drops of blue food colouring, beating with a spatula until you get the right shade.

Put a heaped teaspoon of each buttercream on top of a cupcake. Using a small palette knife, spread the buttercreams over the top, marbling both colours together. Then, using the back of a teaspoon, spike the buttercream like waves. Repeat with the remaining cakes.

Colour the fondant icing grey with a little of the black food colouring and shape into small shark fins. Add to the cupcakes and decorate with the sweets as you like.

Index